Living
in the
Village of Grief

In Memory

Rev. Elder Jean White

Axel Schwaigert

with additions and thoughts by Mary Smail

Living
in the
Village of Grief

Learning to understand my grief

Impressum

Bibliografische Information der Deutschen Nationalbibliothek: Die Deutsche Nationalbibliothek verzeichnet diese Publikation in der Deutschen Nationalbibliografie; detaillierte bibliografische Daten sind im Internet über http://dnb.dnb.de abrufbar

.

Herstellung und Verlag: BoD – Books on Demand, Norderstedt

ISBN: 9783757828950

Acknowledgements...III

A special thank you V

Introduction...6

Living in the Village of grief 8

The Dream 8

The Central Square 11

The Town Hall 13

The Pub 15

The Smith-Shop... 18

The Sacred Space 20

The Hospital 22

The Shop 25

The Cemetery... 27

The Oracle 29

Ways leading out of the village..... 31

The Theory...32

The Theory: The dream................................... 36

The Theory: The Central space 37

The Theory: The Town Hall................................ 39

The Theory: The Pub 41

The Theory: The Smith Shop 42

The Theory: The Sacred Space.. 43

The Theory: The Hospital 45

The Theory: The Shop.. 46

The Theory: The cemetery... 47

The Theory: The Oracle... 49

The Theory: The Way leading out of the Village.............................. 50

How to use this model in a Group setting 52

An Embodied Visit to The Village in a group setting 54

About the Authors 74

Acknowledgements

The original version of this book was written as part of my final thesis for my Doctor in Ministry at Episcopal Divinity School in Cambridge/MA/USA. My thesis was on "Communual Grief in Relationship to HIV/AIDS". For that I had to write about the grief theory I was using for the thesis.

I want to thank the EDS community for three incredible years of learning and growth. EDS made me feel welcome as an international student and many people helped me on my way. I learned a new way of doing theology, reconnected to my own academic roots and was able to find creative ways to express my thoughts.

I want to say thanks to the staff and faculty of EDS: Your support made my learning possible and a joy.

Thanks to my fellow students, who freely shared their thoughts, about their own work as well as mine.

Thanks to my Professors, teachers, mentors: Joan M. Martin, guide through the first year; Angela Bauer-Levesque, a German voice in a foreign academic land; Gale Yee, for stopping me on campus to tell my about grief in the Hebrew Bible; Suzanne Ehly, for an incredible course on voice and power; Fredrica Harris Thompsett, and Sheryl Kujawa-Holbrook, for so much wisdom. Thanks to Prof. Kwok Pui-lan, my teacher in Spirituality. She was the one who encouraged me to do something creative! She convinced me that everybody can write boring theoretical texts and that I should find my own way.

A very special thanks goes to Prof. William Kondrath, my Doctor-father. He helped me with great patience, wisdom and guidance through my final thesis. Thank you for a door that was always open, many conversations and even more emails!

Thanks also to my colleagues at Bestattungshaus Haller in Stuttgart for providing the work space and the environment I work in. Much of my experience I have made there. Thanks to Christian and Andrea Haller for giving me time of to work on this book, and my colleagues for doing my part of the work in that time. This book would not have been possible without them. Thank you, Aaron, for proofreading.

Thank you to Jochen Gewecke for being a friend over many, many years and for his wonderful artwork for the cover of this book.

Thank you to my friends, who again and again asked about the manuscript, and encouraged me to finish it. Thank you, Arno, for all your comments. A special thanks goes to my brother Lutz who kept nagging me and to my whole family.

A special thank you

It is one thing to write a text and then file it, hide it securely in some folder, somewhere in a computer. It is another thing altogether to publish it, to put it out there for others to read. I have to thank an incredible, wonderful person who not only gave me the courage to publish this text, but to remind me, pressure me, writing little notes to ask when I would finally work on the manuscript... In short, she is the Godmother of this book. Thank you Mary Smail for being such a friend and persistent voice!

And Mary is more. As a Drama-Therapist she saw the potential in this approach, tried it in group settings, helped me and encouraged me to try it out myself. She is also the Co-author of a part of this: The Oracle is her idea. This important part of the narrative would not be there if it would not be for Marys insight and wisdom.

Thank you Mary: This book is yours as it is mine!

Introduction

Going through grief and mourning is a profound human experience. It is highly individual, but also communal. As we do not live for ourselves and alone, we do not mourn for ourselves and isolated, but together in many different systems of families, friends and strangers. Everybody experiences his/her grief differently and expresses her/his mourning in different ways. Some understand it as a path they have to go down, some as different stages they have to go through. Some see mourning as a list of tasks that have to be worked through; some just see an overwhelming single task in front of them that with time becomes less overwhelming. Grief and mourning can be understood in different ways. It can be seen as a psychological problem that needs therapeutical help. It can be also understood as a human problem, that best is addressed with the methods of self-help. Or it can be understood as a spiritual experience that needs guidance and/or counselling.

The following model can be understood as both self-help and a proposal for counselling. The story, the explanations and the guiding questions can be read to understand one's own grief and mourning better. It can also help to gain an understanding of the grief and mourning of others, which might be so totally different from our own. In this sense it can be understood as a method of self-help. It also could be used in a one-to-one counselling situation or a counselling group. Here it could serve as a method to facilitate communication about grief and mourning, hopefully leading to a deeper understanding.

The story was purposely not designed in a particular religious or Christian framework. It is not an attempt to explain life and death spiritually. It is an attempt to help people to understand their own grief and the experience of grief of others.

The narrative can be read and used by itself, without the need of further theoretical explanations. For many people, especially when this model is used in a group, this might be enough. People connect to the different places and buildings in the narrative intuitively and fill those places with their own experiences and meaning. Others might want to reflect on the different situations in a more theoretical way. The second part of this book offers some reflections on the different places. This might be helpful for some but can be especially important for those leading this model in a group setting.

The questions after each part of the narrative are an invitation to start to think about those places. Some of them might help; some might not be important at a specific moment at all. They can be used for personal reflection or starting points for a conversation.

Living in the Village of grief

THE DREAM

After many weeks I finally could sleep again and woke up in a dream. I found myself in a deep forest, surrounded by darkness. Tall trees stood around me, blocking out the sky and sun. I did not know, if it was day or night, I was caught in the grey of dusk or dawn. There was no path, no way around me, no way to go, but I started to walk, wandering aimlessly in the forest of my grief and loss. I was alone, had no place to go, no reason to walk. My bare feet felt the stones and the rough ground, every step hurt. My hands, my face, my body felt the thorns and the hard twigs and the burning leaves. No part of my self was whole, everything hurt. So I walked for a long, endless time, in loss and grief, in sorrow and loneliness.

Then the forest thinned, and I stepped out into open space. Soft grass led me down towards a little village of small houses nestled in a valley around a central square. Slowly I walked towards the houses. I could see the light in the windows, smell the smoke from the chimneys, could feel the peace. As I approached, I saw people coming towards me, smiling, greeting me.

"Welcome," they said. "Welcome in your place of grief. Here you can be, you can grieve, here you can stay and be." I did not understand what they meant. Had I not already walked a long way in sorrow and pain, was I not hurt enough? Should I live forever here, in this village of grief? They smiled at me, and said: "Come along, we will show you where you are." And they lead me by the hand into the village, towards the central square. On the way I saw people who I seemed to know. My heart told me, that those people where part of my life, but I could not see them clearly, through the tears in my eyes.

"This is your village of your grief." I heard, "everything you experience, everything you live, has a place here. After the confusion, the pain, the raw hurt of the forest, after being lost, you are here now. Here are places you can go, with your grief, your anger, your tiredness. You are here with all the others who mourn with you, who grieve with you for your love. Here you and they are free to go where each one of you need to go, sometimes together, sometimes alone. You can go quickly from one place to the other or stay for a long time in one place. You can be together with others, or alone, just as you need it. There is no right or wrong, no correct or incorrect way to do your mourning. No one can tell you, what you need to do; no one can walk your path. You are not alone, yet they might go their own way. Some of the way you will walk together. Some of what you and they will do, you will understand. But there will also be moments, when you will not understand. You will ask why they are not with you, why you feel so different. But here, in this village of your grief you can go, where you need to go. You will be welcome, wherever you go. Stay as long as you want, as long as you need. Let us show you the different places of grief, of mourning and of love."

So I went with them, walking through this place, finding houses and rooms, places for me and for others. I saw the Central Square, the Town Hall, the Smith-Shop, the Hospital, the Pub, the Shop, the Sacred Space and the Cemetery and a Tree.

Questions, about myself:
Whom did I lose? What are the memories I have?
What hurts me most, in my way through the forest of pain?
What is just living my daily live, and what is mourning?
Who is with me in this Village?

Questions, about others:
I know who I have lost. Whom did they lose?
What is their daily life, the necessities of getting on with their jobs and families?
What is their mourning?

Space for my own questions and answers:

_____

_____

_____

THE CENTRAL SQUARE

First my guides led me to the central square. Several old houses nestled around this place, cobblestones paved the ground. There was life, although I could not see the individuals here with me. All I could see was the centre of the square. There was a basin, a wellspring of fresh water, with two, three steps leading up to it. A narrow wall surrounded the pool of water and from several outlets on a central column that rose from its middle, came a constant flow of water. A small bush of red roses grew on one side. It was a peaceful place. But the most surprising of all was the central column. On the top, there was a statue. At first I did not recognise it. I thought that the light of the sun was playing tricks with my eyes. But then I saw: it was the beautiful image of my loved one, the one I lost.

With tears in my eyes I turned to my guides, wondering, asking.

"Yes," they said, "you see it right. It is your loved one, the one you mourn. This is you place, and here your loved one is at the centre of it all. All your tears, the tears of sorrow and the tears of joy flow form this fountain, and your tears water the roses of your love. Here is the centre of your grieving, and you can return here as often as you like. From here you can go to all the other places. Here you can remember, here you can love. Do not be afraid, that the memory will fade. Others will meet you here, and you will share your memories with theirs. Your heart will see your loved one here, even if your eyes will should tire. Nobody can take this statue away, and you can keep it here, in the centre, forever."

Questions, about myself:

Who are my guides?

Who leads me in my mourning?

Who can help me in this time?

Where can I find support?

Where can I find my loved one today?

Can I tell him or her about the things I have done today?

Is it good for me to meet with others to share memories?

Or is it still to painful?

Can I ask and invite others to share their memories?

Questions, about others:

What are their memories?

Are they willing to share?

Or is it still to painful?

Do they ask and invite me to share my memories?

Space for my own questions and answers:

_____

_____

_____

THE TOWN HALL

Next, my guides led me to a building nearby. They looked at me with love and sorrow in their eyes. "This is a place, where you will have to go, now and in the future.

A place you will need to organise your live without the lost one, without your love. We know, no-one wants to come here. It is perhaps the worst place of all. The papers you will have to fill out, the decisions you will have to make: Shall you stay or shall you move? And where are all the papers, all the documents you need? You never did that, never did it alone! All the decisions you shall make! You don't know if you can do it, even if you want to do it!

And worst of all, we know, you do not want to even think about the future. But still, there will be a future. A future for the next hours, the next days and years. And that perhaps is the most difficult thing to accept."

He laid his arm around my shoulder, leading me further on my path and said: "Come, there is more to see, and no decisions to make now."

Questions, about myself:

What are the decisions I have to make?

Which ones are urgent; have to be made at once?

Which ones should I wait some more?

How do the others react to my decisions, and why do they react that way?

Who can give me advice?

What is it that I want for my future?

Questions, about others:

What are the decisions the others have to make?

How do I react to their decisions, and why do I react that way?

Space for my own questions and answers:

_____

_____

_____

THE PUB

We then came to a place where I could hear laughter and joy coming from the door. A warm light shone from the windows, and I saw people coming and going. I saw friends shaking hands, smiling at each other, they laughed and joked. I could sense happiness, the community, the absolute opposite of what I felt. There was nothing of the loneliness I lived in. First, I wanted to turn, wanted to be angry! What was this place of happiness, of joy? And why was it here, in my village of grief? How could they dare to be so full of life, so full of joy, when my loved one was no more? I wanted to turn to my guides, angry, full of rage. Why did they show me this, why torment me with something I could not have anymore?

But then I stopped. I did not turn but watched. I saw with desire in my heart this place, and everything in me longed to be part of it. To stop feeling the grief, for just a moment, forget my loss, for just a minute, that was, what I wanted. Be part of life, once more. Suddenly I wanted to feel my body, my heart, my soul once more. I wanted to go in and celebrate. I did not care that I did not feel anything like celebrating. Just to be among those people, friends, in joy, like we had been together so often before.

Tears came in my eyes. I did not know what to feel anymore. Longing and loss fought in my heart. I felt a hand on my shoulder, comforting, and one of my guides spoke: "My friend, this place is also part of your village of grief. Your longing for life, as well as the reality that others might want to celebrate and be joyful. Their grief might be different from yours. They will not have forgotten, they still might grieve, but life goes on, and days of joy will come. The circle of the year will bring the seasons of joy, and the ordinary day will bring unexpected laughter. Don't be angry with them when they will need this time of rest from grief and mourning. And don't judge yourself, when you will enjoy these times of rest and refreshment yourself. It is part of your grief. You might come and stay for a while. Let your friends and family relieve you for a moment of your pain. Bring your loved one in your heart and memory with you, remember the good times, before you step out of this place once more."

Questions, about myself:

What makes me impatient?
What can I do to make space for others?

What are my needs?
What are especially difficult times? During the day? The Week? The Year?
How can I prepare for those times?

Questions, about others:

How can we combine expressions of life?

What could be the reasons for them to laugh?

What are their expressions of grief?

How can I make room for their expressions of grief?

How can I communicate my needs, and my feelings?

Space for my own questions and answers:

_____

_____

_____

THE SMITH-SHOP

Already from far away I could hear where we were going. The sound of hammers, ringing high in the air, the beating of metal on hot metal welcomed us.

"What shall I do in the smithy?" I shouted in the ear of my guide. "I never worked with iron in my life!" "Yes," she answered, smiling, "Yes, I know. But still, this is your place of work. Where you really can beat it, hammer it out, sweat, be angry and even violent! Here you can work out all that you need to do, the hard work, the painful work. To this place you can come, when you feel that sitting around is not enough. When your body and your soul cry out for action, you can come here and take the hammer, and swing it."

I saw the hot fire, saw the tools, and saw all the work I wanted to do. I saw what I needed to do, for myself and for others. Today I was too tired to start. I knew that today that hammer would be too heavy. But I also knew that perhaps tomorrow I would come back, take up the chore, and with tears and joy would work.

Questions, about myself:
What is it I need to do?
Why am I doing it?
Why am I not doing it?

Questions, about others:

What do they need to do?

Why are they doing it?

Why are they not doing it?

Space for my own questions and answers:

_____

_____

_____

THE SACRED SPACE

We entered a large, quiet building. Stillness and serenity welcomed us into the soft light of candles and the warm colours of stained glass windows. There seemed to be music in the air, though I could not tell, where it came from, nor what it was. We sat down on one of the benches, sat there for what seemed to be forever. A deep feeling of peace filled my heart, more peace than I ever knew, a peace and quietness that brought tears into my eyes.

Without any words I understood, what my guides wanted to show me here. Here was the quiet place, the place to meditate. Here I could search for meaning in my life. Here I could think, free of all the chores that filled my days. Here I could even rest and sleep, and dream the pain away. And here I could listen, listen to my heart and to that music of my soul.

Perhaps one day I could even come and pray. Pray all on my sorrow and pray my pain away. And perhaps those prayers could find an answer, perhaps there was somebody out there who would listen, feel, and respond. Today I did not know what to believe. But still, the place, the time, was holy.

Questions, about myself:

Where can I find places of quietness for me?

When are my times of quietness?

Can I and do I want to share those places and times with others?

How can I set boundaries for my quiet space and time?

Questions, about others:

Where are their places of quietness?

Do I want to invite them into my quiet space and time?

What can I do to honour their quiet time and space?

Space for my own questions and answers:

_____

_____

_____

THE HOSPITAL

I could smell the next building, before I could really see it. It was the antiseptic, sick smell of a hospital. Green walls in long hallways where every step has an echo and everyone only speaks in hushed voices. I knew this smell, these sounds all too well. The memories of endless hours rose from my heart.

"This is not only a place for painful memories. It is also a place for you. Many things in you need healing. You are hurt, in body, mind and soul. Take your time to feel your wounds, to acknowledge them, to let them heal. This will take time, and you will have to take good care of yourself. This is not something that happens by itself. In the time of grief sometimes your body does not speak clearly to you. You might forget to eat, to drink. You might eat and drink too much. You have to be your caretaker, your nurse, and take good care of yourself."

We started to walk down one of the long corridors, and I saw people being nursed, and cared for. Others sat next to them and listened, as they told of their wounds and aches and pains. I saw doctors thinking about the correct treatment, and nurses who brought what was needed. In one room I watched, as they removed a heavy bandage, looking carefully at the wound. And I watched, as surprise replaced hopelessness in the eyes and on the face of the patient, as she saw, that the wound had started to heal.

"And you will find others here as well, here in this place of pain and healing," said my guide, "who are walking wounded, like yourself. There are times when you need to know your own pain, your own wound, to understand how others are in pain. And sometimes not the doctor, nor a nurse, no medicine and no hospital can help, but rather those who grieve and suffer with you. They are the ones who have the patience to watch you get better. They are wounded healers."

I knew, that I had to come here often, for myself and for my healing.

Questions, about myself:

Do I take care of myself?

Do I eat, drink and sleep properly?

What do I need for my body?

What do I need for my spirit?

What do I need for my soul?

Where are my wounds?

Where could I find help to heal?

Questions, about others:

Where are they hurt and wounded?

What can be helpful for them?

What do they do for their healing?

Space for my own questions and answers:

_____

_____

_____

THE SHOP

We stood in front of a little shop. It seemed that it was one of those little places that are horrible overcrowded, but where you could find everything. Where a nice old lady served you in your childhood and never let you go without a candy, taken from a large jar on the counter. It was one of those places that nowadays is only a memory.

Of course, there needs to be a shop in this village, I thought. Where else should one get all those things one needs? But then I hesitated: What did I need? What did I desire? The few things for my daily life I had, and more I did not need. I did not want to go shopping, not ever anymore.

"We know," said my guide. "But this is not an ordinary shop. This is the shop where you can get your things for life, the things you need. Here you can find that new flat, and that new job. That smaller car and those smaller pots and pans to make meals just for one. Here you can find those things you wanted to do for so long but couldn't. Here you find addresses of groups and meeting places, of help and support. Here you can find all things you need."

I understood but said: "I do not want to find anything new. Why should I? Life has stopped. Why should I buy new things, find new places? I do not need anything; I do not want to go anywhere. There is no reason to go anywhere anymore."

"Yes," said my guide, "the life you knew, the life you loved, has stopped, has come to an end. But your life itself has not stopped. Your life goes on. It is different, now. And therefore, you will need different things; you will have to find a new meaning, new ways. And so, it is all right to come here, to go out to shop, to find new things. Some of them you need, and some of them you might just want. You want them, because they are good for you and you will enjoy them. All of it you can find here."

Questions, about myself:

What do I really want?
What do I really need?
Do I know where to find it?

Questions, about others:

What do they need?
What are the reasons, why they act and buy and live as they do?

Space for my own questions and answers:

_____

_____

_____

THE CEMETERY

We then came to a place where it grew dark. A heavy iron gate guarded the entrance, a high wall reached from horizon to horizon. Ivy grew among the bars of the gate. Under dark skies I could hear the calling of an owl, flying under the low branches of a weeping willow. I felt the cold, could feel the thorns of the forest in my skin. I knew this place. At the day of my loss it became my home, too. We stood at the gates of the cemetery. I knew: here was my love and here I buried all my hopes, my dreams, my joy, my laughter. So often I had already been here, during the day, and now in my dreams. Fear surrounded me.

Tears filled my eyes, I could not speak, not hear. I sat down next to the grave, where I wanted to bury myself. A long time we sat, in sobbing silence.

Then my guide spoke. "Yes, cry and grieve. Let no one tell you, that you have to leave this place. It is a dark place, yes, a place of mourning and of fear, of unknown horrors hiding in the darkness between the graves. You have to come here, even if it is hard. You have to come here and meet your fears and all that scares you, in death and life. Because only if you come here, and see what it is that scares and frightens you, can you deal with it. You can fight it, work it through. Yes, you can go to sunnier places, but then you have to return and do your work. For if you do not find your grief and fear, it will find you, haunt you, torment you. This cemetery can be a good and comforting place, a place of memories, but also a place of struggle."

Questions, about myself:
Where is my cemetery?
What do I fear?
How can I confront my fears?
What helps me in my mourning?

Questions, about others:
Where are their cemeteries?
What do they fear most?
What are they doing to confront their fears?
What is helpful for them?

Space for my own questions and answers:

_____

_____

_____

THE ORACLE

After wandering a while we found ourselves in a quiet garden. There were no walls to guard it, yet it felt guarded and sheltered, a place of rest. It was open and full of surprises, more a dream than any garden I had ever seen. The sunbeams danced on flowers, who seem to laugh in joyous outbursts of colors. Bees sang their humming song of sweet honey, and the birds filled the air with song and sounds. I looked around to see what I would meet in this garden.

There was a tree, unlike any tree I had ever seen. It was a tree in full bloom of spring, and in the lush green of summer. It was in red and golden leaves of autumn, and bare and covered with the snow of a cold winter night. It was all and more, timeless and full of time. I turned to my guide, but he just smiled, as if I already knew what to see. And then I started to see it, I began to hear. It was all around me, in the beauty of the garden, in the sounds and the smell. And out of seeing came hearing. I heard it in the flight of the bird, the color of the leaf, I saw it in the sound of the brook and the wind in the branches. It was like seeing the sound of a promise, a future, a hope. It was like hearing the light of the sun, a whisper of days to come, of love to live. It was a quiet voice, and I knew, without explanation, without any words, that I heard the oracle of times to come, of days not yet here, of hope yet unfelt.

"Yes," my companion said after a while. "You can hear it, it is here for you, in the silence and the sound, in light and darkness. It is what you cannot think and say, but feel. It is what has no words, but meaning. It will tell you, in many ways, that you can see, when you look with your heart."

Questions, just for myself:
Where can I find the stillness in me, to listen to that voice of the future?
What do I hope it will say?
What do I fear it will say?

Space for my own questions and answers:

_____

_____

_____

WAYS LEADING OUT OF THE VILLAGE....

Finally we walked past the houses, left all the places we had visited behind. I got tired and I wanted to rest. I did not want to go back to the forest I had come from, a dream ago. "You may sleep, and rest" I heard my guides say. "But we want to show you one last thing." So I opened my eyes once more and did not see the trees, the forest, I had expected and feared. Instead I saw a path in front of me, leading alongside a small stream, through blooming meadows, over rolling hills past friendly trees.

"We want you to know, that there are ways that lead from this place. They are not for you, yet. And perhaps it will take a long, long time before you will have the strength, or the desire to walk them. Others might walk before you, some will walk with you and others still, will stay behind. You alone can decide when you will go, how far you'll walk, how fast you'll travel. Nobody can tell you when you have to go. Nobody will force you out of this place. For this is your village of grief.

And even if you go, walk one or two or many steps away from here, you can always return, visit the place you need. The doors here are always open, and you are always welcome. But now sleep, and rest, for the next day is near..."
I closed my eyes and slept and woke up in the morning for another day of sorrow, grief and life.

The Theory

"Grief Theories" are often a useful tool to understand grief and mourning in general. They are also often useful for people in the process and experience of grief and mourning to understand what is going on in them, with them and around them. They can help to understand ones own reactions in grief and the reactions of those who are close to oneself. Unfortunately, "Grief Theories" are often very theoretical, dry and not easy to understand, especially in times when mourning is a reality of life, and it is therefore difficult to have the necessary distance from oneself that is necessary for theoretical thinking.

The following serves only to mention the grief theory I base my story on. For this, I work with the dual process model of coping with bereavement by Margaret and Wolfgang Stroebe.

This model allows a lot of freedom of individual expressions and experiences of grief and mourning. It describes two main areas that a grieving persons experiences: The "Loss orientated" area and the "restoration oriented" area. Loss orientated are fears, regret, sadness, hopelessness, isolation, feelings of guilt, the preference to dwell in memories, acknowledgement of grief, mourning. Restoration orientated are feelings like hopefulness, gratefulness, the desire to move on, the making of plans, looking into the future, hunger for normality. This part also indcludes the taking time off from grief and the fact that the grieving person is able to function.

In this model, the grieving person moves both freely between and within those two main areas. Sometimes this movement can be very rapidly changing from one place to the other, sometimes the grieving person remains over a long period of time in one area or sub-area. There is no set order or timeframe for this. One can also experience extreme changes from one to the other within very short periods of time. Sometimes people find themselves in two places at once, as impossible that might sound.

Therefore, this model is extremely helpful in looking at groups of grieving people. It allows the different individuals to position themselves at any given time at a specific place in this model. They can do this without needing to expect the others within the grieving group to be at the same emotional, intellectual or spiritual point. This model explains therefore very clearly why and how various individuals can experience grief very differently and live out their mourning in very different ways. They are just in a different space within this model.

"Living in the village of grief" is an attempt to bring this model in the form of a narrative, finding different creative spaces for the different subcategories of the two main areas. Those different imaginative spaces tend to be situated more in one area than the other. But they all include elements of both. That means that if two persons find themselves in the same place, they still can have different experiences of that place.

"Living in the village of grief" presents a narrative that gives a visual and imaginative background to different experiences of grief and mourning. The readers are invited to identify themselves and their experience in this narrative. This can help to identify one's own place in the larger experience of loss, grief and mourning. And the readers then might be able to identify where others are in their experience of grief and mourning. Very often people grieve together for the same loss, but they do it in different pace or different intensity.

Although to grieve is a highly individual experience, it is nevertheless an experience that happens with others. Especially in families, this duality of the individual and the communal often leads to conflict. Different people deal with their grief differently, they mourn differently. What is appropriate and helpful for one, might look highly inappropriate and even irreverently to others. One might need a lot of quiet time to learn to understand the loss, needs a lot of time where nothing changes. Another might feel the need to be hyperactive, change a lot in the own life. Some people want to keep as much of the possessions of the deceased around for as long as possible, others might want to clean out everything as soon as possible, for everything is loaded with painful memories. There is no right or wrong in this, just difference. The story might serve as an explanation for this experience and hopefully as a way to communicate the own experience.

Grief is not a single experience one has to go through, but it is a highly complex mixture of very different, often contradictory experiences. And there is also no real end to it. The acute phase of grief and mourning will finish at one time, but the experience of grief will remain, as the loss will remain. The experience of grief will change over time. And as the grief changes, the needs change.

The different places and buildings in the village of grief are symbols for those different needs and moods in our mourning. There is no set order in which we have to visit them; we might not even visit them all. In some places we will stay for a very long time, others we will leave quickly. In some we will be once, and never again, others we will visit very often. And as time goes by, different places will become differently important. All those places and buildings are invitations to go to, stay when we need it. And perhaps find new and other places that are just for us, are our own invention. This model is not a closed system but an open model, where everybody can find and create their own spaces.

THE THEORY: THE DREAM

To lose a loved one is a terrible experience. Expected or unexpected, nothing can prepare us for this situation. Suddenly we find ourselves in the overwhelming situation of grief and mourning, where nothing is clear, where one is in shock, where one finds oneself bruised and hurt. At the beginning, mourning is like walking through an endless forest. A place without light, where day and night have lost their meaning, where everything hurts and cuts, burns, and bruises us. We hurt and at the same time we are numb, unable to feel anything, except that loss.

Grief and mourning is a very complex and individual experience. There is no grief that is exactly the same as the other. No two people experience the same loss. Although the same person has passed away, it is not the same person for them that mourn. It is the wife or the husband for one, the father or the mother for others, the sister, the brother, the friend again for others. Therefore, grief and mourning will be different for all. So, everybody will experience his or her own grief, will mourn in his or her own way. Men and women will mourn differently; singles and those in close circles of families and friends will mourn differently; young and old will mourn differently. And everyone will make his or her own experiences.

But grief and mourning is also something that usually happens in relationship to others. There are other people around you, that grieve and mourn themselves. Every one of those persons around you does

this in their own way and at their own pace, with their own expressions.
Sometimes those expressions of grief of different people are compatible
and go along together very well. Sometimes they are so different from
our own experience, that we cannot understand it. Sometimes that
leads to irritation, because they are at a different place, sometimes it
even leads to conflict, when we cannot understand why the other does
or say things we do not expect, or that hurt us. Or the opposite, that
they do not do and say things, we want them to do or say.

It is therefore important to think about your own grief, to find out what
it is that I need, and also think about, where the other might be in the
same moment. We have to find places where several people can be
together, and others where I can be alone, perhaps need to be alone.
Sometimes we even change quickly, within moments, from one place
to the other. Our moods and needs can change, and sometimes it is
not even clear, why they change. Not even for ourselves.

THE THEORY: THE CENTRAL SPACE

The love for the one that is lost is in the centre of all that we feel. The
fact that he or she is no longer here, no longer part of our live is the
central experience. And the love is still there. Every tear of grief and
sorrow that we shed is also a tear of love. Only where there was love,
can there now be grieving and mourning. The love did not stop with

our loss, the love will stay. How we live our love will change, but not the love itself.

And we do not have to give up that love, surrender it to memory. We can still keep and live and feel that love as a reality of life. For our loved one is still part of us, still part of our own experience of life. We do not have to give up or let go of this love. No-one, nothing can force us to give up, or say farewell to that love forever. Our love can stay in our hearts. It has to find a new place, though. We cannot stay in the place of our memory forever, freezing everything into a everlasting moment in time. As hard as it is, we have to continue to live, leave that museum of our memories. But we can take those memories, that love, and our loved one with us, into our life.

The reason for our grief does not exclusively have to be the loss of a loved one, another human being. The reason for grief can be very individual. It can be the experience of the loss of a job, a specific position in life; the loss of a pet; the loss of one's youth. It can be the realisation of the loss of possibilities and opportunities. All those losses can be the reason for the experience of grief. And they are all valid experiences. Unfortunately, different types of losses are valued differently. The loss of a pet seems to be "less than" the loss of a partner. But sometimes the loss of a beloved animal, who has been a faithful companion over many years, can be a deeper loss than the loss of a partner that was emotionally distant for an even longer time. The loss of a job can be opportunities for one person, but for the other mean the total loss of meaning in life, of being needed, of the source of one's experience of self-worth.

For the following I tend to use examples that occur when a person has passed away. That is not meant to dimmish the other experiences of grief, but I assume that those examples are easy to relate to.

THE THEORY: THE TOWN HALL

When we lose a loved one, almost immediately we have to make decisions. Often, we have to organise funerals and make arrangements for a grave. Immediately we have to deal with forms and documents, which we often have never seen before. In a moment of shock and confusion we have to decide on things that often cannot be changed later. A gravesite stays where we decided it should be, even if we move.

In the weeks and months after the loss we have to make a lot of those decisions. Some might come easy for us, because we have made those kinds of decisions all the time. Some might be very difficult to make, because we never had to make those decisions in our live. And sometimes the smallest decisions are the hardest: "What shall I eat tonight?" can be a huge problem for someone who was used his/her entire live, that this decision was made for them. Decisions that seem very small to one can be huge for others. Sometimes the largest decisions come very easy: "I will sell the house and move" can appear to be a big decision to others but might have already be made long before the loss, and now is only executed. Decisions that seem life changing and big for one, can be small and easy to make for others.

All those decisions take a lot of energy, the small ones as well as the large ones. All of them add up to the feeling of being overwhelmed. It is therefore very important, to recognise those decisions as something important, and something that has to be done in its own time.

Sometimes this decision-making process leads to tension and conflict in a group of grieving individuals. Not all the decisions are valued the same by different people, and the timing can vary. Some people make decisions quickly, others take a long time.

In grief and mourning we therefore should be patient with each other, recognising the difficulty in making decisions and show understanding. We should help each other in making those decisions. And we should always stop and think about the reasons the other might have, before we start to criticise.

THE THEORY: THE PUB

Grief and mourning is a complex and difficult experience. It is not something one does for a set period of time and, after having completed it, continues with one's normal life. The loss of a loved one changes everything. It is therefore often very difficult to understand, that other people will go back to their normal life, while we are still in the middle of our time of mourning. To see others to continue with life or, even worse, enjoying themselves is a very painful experience that can often lead to conflict. We find it difficult to understand, that others laugh and enjoy themselves. We are angry with them, and we are envious and often angry with ourselves for feeling this way, because of course we know that they cannot live our grief, that they cannot do our mourning.

Especially in families with children this can lead to stress and conflict. The little grandchildren for example might know, that Granny passed away in January, but for them this is half a lifetime ago. And now they want to celebrate Christmas, they want their presents, they want to celebrate. For them it does not make sense, that Grandpa is sad, cries and gets impatient. They do not understand that for him this is the first Christmas without his wife in over 40 years. And sometimes adults can be children, too.

It requires a lot of patience and compassion on both sides.
To accept that people are in different positions and moments can be very difficult. It is possible that the other has a different path altogether.

It also can be that they only need a short break from their grief, or that they have just learned to live with the demands of the calendar, work, their social status, and the necessities of social life.

It is difficult to watch others live and celebrate. It is even more difficult to feel it in oneself. This need to be with others, to not be alone for a while; to join in their happiness for just a moment; to allow ourselves to laugh, in the middle of our tears. This can be very difficult: to laugh even when our loved one is no more.

But it is a reality of life, that those lighter moments are a part of our life, too. And therefore, we have to be patient with ourselves and allow ourselves those moments of rest. We can be together, and celebrate in joy with our friends without forgetting our love. The same patience we grant our grandchildren, we can sometimes grant ourselves.

THE THEORY: THE SMITH SHOP

To grieve and mourn is hard work. Not only regarding actual things, like decisions and preparations that one has to do in the event of a loss. But also in the emotional work that has to be done. Different people react very differently to the experience of loss. Some become literally paralysed, not able to do even the smallest things; others become overly active, feel the need to work and do things. Some have to work day and night to cope with this stress. This can lead to very painful moments, especially in families when one part of the family feels the need for quietness, of not changing anything, and another part of the family wants to work. Sometimes people start immediately after the loss, often even before the funeral, to clean out wardrobes and cupboards, pack up clothings and give it away. These activities are than experienced as insensitive by others, they are experienced as an attempt to forget, or get the memory out of the way. Often it is neither of those, but simply the need to do something, to be active in a situation where we cannot really do anything anymore. It can be a symbol of regaining and exercising control over the situation.

Some people return to their daily work very quickly. To go back to work, to do something, sometimes to return to a routine, or do something that has some kind of meaning for them, is part of their grieving, their way of working it through.

THE THEORY: THE SACRED SPACE

This Sacred Space is not necessarily a place about faith, but of peace and quietness. For many in western culture, this Sacred Space will be visualised as a church building. But most certainly this Sacred Space is not about a particular faith or creed. Some people have clear ideas of faith and can express their faith in clear words, even in times of loss and mourning. Some find a lot of strength and consolation in their faith.

Their churches, temples, mosques or synagogues are very real places to go to and feel connected to a higher power and their inner being. Some people cannot and don't want to express their faith. They have more questions than answers, especially in this time.

And others feel nothing but hate and rage and anger towards God in all of God's forms and even more towards God's representatives on earth.

Sometimes we have all those experiences right there within ourselves. It is part of our being human, our humanness, that we ask those ultimate questions: Where do we come from? Where will we go? Why me? And ultimately: Why?

We all ask those questions. Some ask them louder than others, some ask them sooner, others later. We usually ask those questions within a framework that we are used to. Others will have different frameworks. And we can only ask those questions ourselves and find answers for ourselves. We cannot force others to think and ask them, too and find the same answers we do. But we can invite others to listen, when we ask, and we can open ourselves up to listen to what they tell us.

THE THEORY: THE HOSPITAL

Very often the hospital in our real life is a place full of painful memories. We have spent hours by the bed of a loved one, saw him/her in suffering and in pain, and eventually pass away. It is often the very smell and the typical sounds of a hospital that throw us right back into that horrible time, even after years.

But Hospitals are also places of healing. When we lose a loved one, we are hurt and wounded and it takes a lot of time to heal those wounds. This hurt and those wounds can be very physical. A long time spent caring for a sick and dying loved one can leave our bodies tired, weary and unwell. Part of our grieving therefore means that we have to take care of our own body. This is not in addition to our grieving, but part of our grieving and mourning itself.
Even if we are not hurt physically, grief has a physical dimension. It can lead to problems with sleeping or, in the oppositely, to an overwhelming tiredness. Our body reacts to grief, and we have to listen to it if we do not want to hurt our bodies even more.

Sometimes though, especially during the first time experiencing grief, our bodies do not tell us clearly what they need. This happens especially in the time between the actual death and the funeral, but also often in the time thereafter. Ours bodies don't feel hunger or thirst, we feel numb. It is therefore very important, that we consciously eat and drink. We have a responsibility for our bodies, even and especially in our grief.

The same is true for our mental and spiritual side. There can be deep wounds there. This can be anger that he/she died and left us alone. This can be anger towards others, who could not prevent that death, or might even have caused it. All those hurts and wounds are real and important. We have to examine them carefully and think about how we can heal them. This healing can mean a better understanding of what happened, and can mean gaining a certain distance to parts of what transpired, or can lead to forgiving others and sometimes forgiving even ourselves. All of that can take a very long time and is a very difficult part of our grieving.

THE THEORY: THE SHOP

It is a reality, that the loss of a loved one often comes with other profound changes in our life. Not only did our status in the family change, but often the circumstances of our lives change, too. We have to think about moving form a large house that suited two, to a smaller place. We have to move, perhaps to be closer to family, or take that step into retirement, now. Sometimes we have to get a job to support our family.

Some of us might need to obtain professional help, in therapy or just for the daily chores. We need a new car, or have to learn to use public transport. We have to learn new skills and have to reorganise our life. Often it is the seemingly simple things in life that are the most difficult.

If someone never had to use a washer and dryer, that new skill can be very difficult to learn. And all learning takes energy. And this energy is often not available.

These things we need are very important, and it is necessary that we think about them carefully. It is part of grieving to think about one's own life and future.

THE THEORY: THE CEMETERY

For some people the cemetery and the grave are or become very important places. They visit the grave every day; they feel that they have a special connection to their loved one, here, at the grave. Sometimes this cemetery is not even a real place, but a place inside. It is a place of memories, of reconnection, a place where we can feel very close to our loved one. Sometimes this place can be a picture on the wall, with whom we talk. Or the empty chair, that will remain forever his or hers. It can be a place where we can see our loved one sitting with us, during long and lonely evenings.

All who grieve and mourn have those places. For some it is very important to visit the actual gravesite regularly. For others it might be an utter meaningless place, where nothing of the loved one remains. In every group of mourning people, there are different cemeteries, sometimes as many as there are people involved. And it is very often not the actual, real cemetery.

If someone does not visit the grave or the cemetery regularly, it does not mean, that this person does not grieve. They might just have another place. And it might be helpful to find out where the other goes to grieve, inside or outside. Perhaps we can come along one day.

The Cemetery is also a symbol for our fears. When we experience loss, we are confronted with a lot of fears as well. We have to face our own mortality; we experience fear of the future; we do not know if we "can make" it; a lot of seemingly little things scare us: to use the washer and dryer, to fill out bank forms, to deal with daily life. All that and much more scares us, sometimes even paralyse us. Part of the grieving is to deal with those fears. Some have to be addressed by simply learning to do it: reading the user manual and washing clothing for the first time, for example. Some need professional help. But all of them need to be dealt with; otherwise, they will not go away and scare us forever.

What seems very scary to one can be very easy to others. Here lies a great danger and an opportunity for grieving groups of friends or families. The danger is to underestimate the level of difficulty a certain situation has for the other, and dismiss it as not difficult enough. Or one assumes, that everything that is difficult for oneself is equally as difficult for the other. This can lead to deep conflict. The task is to find out what the other needs and help each other.

THE THEORY: THE ORACLE

It is in the real sense of the word a place outside even of the imagination. It is this moment beyond words, that even now defies explanation. It is a kind of open space which is hard to see unless you have eyes that see in the darkness.

If you come towards it there is a gift waiting for you. You will be met here in a half seeing way. The being or thing that you lost will find you there. Nothing and nobody is totally lost. There is always memory and the feeling of longing, that keeps it close to us. And even the gap a loss leaves behind remains.

They are waiting. They will not meet you during the everyday – they will meet you in a song that you hear. Or a half-formed image. Or a dream. It may be that a bird catches your attention, comes close and watches you. Or that a feather drops from the sky. It may be a felt sense of the beloved or a message you need to hear from the thing you have lost, suddenly takes up residence in you. Your brain may not compute it but your skin and soul recognize it. It may be a tingle, a vibration, a sound. Come to the oracle ready to hear – what do you hear? What can be half seen? And will you let the eyes of imagination take you one step closer to that sensation.

We often do not have ways of communicating about those moments or encounters. Especially the very rationalistic western culture often dismisses those moments as imaginary or superstitious. Yet as for all other experience of grief, those experiences, too, are real for the one who experiences them, and they should be treated as such.

THE THEORY: THE WAY LEADING OUT OF THE VILLAGE

This is a difficult concept to understand but is essentially important. Most people in grief will experience this: There is a life after grief. For some it will appear as a goal of the process of grieving, and they will walk towards it. For others it seems to be an impossible goal, and they fear that they will never reach it. Both are possible. Most people will experience a change in their grief, an integration of the loss and the grief itself into the reality of life. This is what happens in the majority of all cases after some period of time. Normal life will come back, sleep, the ability to eat again, the ability to even smile and laugh again: all will return. The experience of grief will change, quantitatively for some, qualitatively for others. The sense of grief and loss will never be gone completely, though. Yet it will become a part of one's own life, experience, and personality. Loss and grief will change one's own outlook on reality and ultimately it will change one's personality. One will be another person upon leaving the village of grief. Some even see it as an experience of growth.

There are two things to be aware of, though. First: There is no real timeline to this process. It can be a short process or a long one. It very much depends on the situation and the personality of the person grieving. It is not possible to set a certain time limit for oneself. And one cannot set a time limit for others. And it is possible, normal, and even advisable to revisit one's own grief from time to time.

There are situations and personalities that need more support than others. There are times when grief becomes unbearable, unmanageable. If this is the case, please ask for help. Do not hesitate to ask for counselling or therapy! It is a sign of strength to ask for help, not a sign of weakness.

Please ask your medical advisor for institutions in your community that can help you. You do not have to do this all alone. Let others, professionals, help you, if you feel that this is necessary in your situation!

How to use this model in a Group setting

The first version of this book was written for an academic project at Episcopal Divinity School in Cambridge/MA/USA. At first it was not more of that. It was originally not intended to be used in personal grief or in a group setting. Thanks to a very dear friend, Mary Smail, it grew into something much more beautiful. Thanks to her there is this book today. As a trained and experienced Drama Therapist she has a deep understanding of how to bring the Village to life. I am very grateful that she agreed to contribute the following chapter to our book.

The Village of Grief has no set path you have to walk through. One can wander freely from one place to the other, just as one needs it.

The same is true for a Group setting. Different Groups might need different orders, in which the story is told. Except for the Dream and The Ways out of the Village, the order of places can be exchanged. We would not recommend leaving out any of the places, though.

Those places are the most basic experiences of grief and mourning. They are, though, written from the perspective of a white, middle class, middle age, academically trained male. They are written in a Western European cultural framework. As a Group leader, please feel free to add places that are culturally important and relevant. One suggestion that has been brought, was a beauty salon. And I have to thank Prof. Dr. Kondrath for this insight. In many cultures a beauty salon offers a safe space for women to gather. Here they can gather without the pressure of male dominated society to communicate freely. As a man I cannot write and describe the possibilities, challenges, and questions of such a place. Let the group find and invent their own places, if necessary and relevant.

An Embodied Visit to The Village in a group setting

By Mary Smail

I was introduced to The Village of Grief in a small family church setting. We had lost a vital congregation member and were in deep mourning and premature and unexpected rupture. What had once been safe had become traumatised and emptied. There was no comfort, and as a small group of people, all we could do was cling together in our bereavement, refusing shortcuts to repair. We desperately needed to grieve.

We heard that Dr Axel Schwaigert, a priest in our denomination living in Germany, had just finished his thesis on death and loss, so we asked him to come to us and tell us about what he had found. Axel talked to us, firstly about the theory of loss and psychological models offering ideas about stages of the bereavement process, and then he told us about The Village.

As someone who was particularly traumatised by this loss, we were all in, visiting The Village gave me an entirely new way of perceiving and respecting my grief. The Village allowed imagination to come into the loss journey, as I was permitted to explore my deep sadness creatively. There was no timeline or sense of working through sequential stages of mourning. Seeing my bereavement through a metaphor allowed me to go in and out of grief as my soul so deeply required. It had a circular quality, letting me go with my loss experience as and when I wanted. The Village honoured the different waves that grieving and mourning bring, allowing me to visit the various emotions I needed to express daily. It accommodated all I was experiencing in a non-linear, poignant, and honouring way. But more than that!

When Axel visited us and described each of the locations in The Village, the Dramatherapist in me woke up. Dramatherapy works from the premise that when we embody images, they come alive because the body's somatic responses are a means of intelligence beyond what only our left brain can think. I began to consider how a bereavement experience could be shared in a group of people, working and playing together so that a collective intention could be recognised and shared and a currency of loss-suffering could be openly met, rather than being silenced or hidden away from everyday life.

Loss is profoundly disallowed in western society. Society gives a few weeks after someone dies and then another two weeks maximum, after the funeral. Then the expectation is that the bereaved being gets 'back to normal and moves on with life. Loss doesn't work like that. We do not go back to who we were. When we are in loss, we are no longer who we were. The Village honours the ongoing journey we make as we struggle to return to life and live it differently.

I set about to explore how The Village could be shared in a group of people and experimented with using it with professionals working in bereavement, trainee counsellors at the Re-Vision Psychotherapy and

Counselling in London. We worked in an embodied way face to face in a group, and I also presented it to people worldwide using the Zoom platform. I shared my work consistently with Axel and slightly adapted it to meet what is needed when working through therapeutic improvisation and story enactment.

Rather than using the image of Axel's dream, I devised the idea of facilitating the work by casting the facilitator as The Tour Guide. I invited people to participate in an imaginative embodied trip to The Village, just as might happen when you visit a location and explore it as a tourist.

I stressed that this was not about performance but that each group member would be supported to work at their own comfort level when using movement work. People could use the whole room for their exploration, but they could choose to do this minimally, finding a spot in the room to work from or even staying seated and work more privately from that place. This must be named and agreed – each person needs to find their own comfort with this way of working and some skill in holding this is essential. An example of a session and the script I have adapted now follows.

Before the session

Ask people to bring a piece of material – no bigger than a travelling rug, no smaller than a towel, in any material you like.

Pen and paper – crayons if you like to use these

The Session – Going to The Village

Focus

Welcome people and invite them to share their names and a sentence on why they have come.

After speaking, ask them to share a gesture to sum up, what brings them.

Other group members mirror this back

Warm Up

Invite people to walk around the space (Music can support this)

Their mission is to play with different ways of travelling, with the facilitator offering suggestions.

Move in a direct way, then the opposite - in a meandering way.

Move firmly with a sense of weight, then move lightly as if you are a feather.

Move with ease and flow, then change to move in a stop/start bound flow form of travelling.

Move close to people, then play with avoiding others and making for the spaces in the room.

Join a partner as the music plays - try to avoid eye contact and pick up the movement from the other person rather than talk.

Travel together – build in pauses, changes of directions etc.

Meet another set of two travellers

Form a movement greeting together

Work in small groups with your cloth

Use your cloth to create:

A meadow, a pathway, a forest, a village green etc.

A few minutes to prepare and then share with the group.

Check out with the people they have worked with and return to their own space

Ask people to find a starting place in the room with their cloth and pen/paper

The Village of Grief Story – tell rather than read if possible

To lose a loved one is a terrible experience. Expected or unexpected, nothing can prepare us for this situation. Suddenly we find ourselves in the overwhelming situation of grief and mourning, where nothing is clear, one is in shock, and one finds oneself bruised and hurt. The first time of mourning is like walking through an endless forest—a place without light, where day and night have lost meaning. We hurt, and at the same time, we are numb, unable to feel anything except that loss.

The Village of Grief buildings symbolizes the different needs and moods in our mourning.

We will visit each of these places today and spend some time there. As we see each location, there will be a short moment to gather your personal and/ or professional reflections on this place, and we can talk about it after the visit. You will only have to share what you want to share. You will be a Traveler to this Village, and when it is needed, I, as your Tour Guide, will let you know when it is time to move on.

Please be ready to begin moving and travelling, as we did a moment ago when we explored the room. I will direct you.

We are going now to The Village.

Beginning the Story

You find yourself on a beautiful day walking through the countryside. It is warm and gentle, and you can feel the sun on your body warming you. You stop to be with this and enjoy the journey.

Then ahead, you see a wooded area and move on towards it. As you come closer, you can see it is an old forest, but you are not daunted and enter. At first, there is a pathway that is easy to follow, but this gets less easy to see as you journey. It becomes dark, and the paths are less clearly marked or visible. You see ahead a clearing and a sign welcoming you as you travel. It says The Village of Grief, and you can see a little village full of buildings ahead.

Find a way to enter the Village... and find your way to the village square where I will meet you.

Give time for people to move

At the centre of the square is a basin, a wellspring of fresh water, with two or three steps leading up to it. A small bush of red roses grows on one side. Most surprising of all, there is a Monument. It is a statue of who or what you have lost – the person or thing you mourn. This is the centre of your grieving, and you can come here any time you like, for as long as you like. No one can take this place from you.

Come into the Village Square with your beloved person there. For a time, you gather the memories of the person or thing you loved, and then when the time is right, you come and lay a rose by the monument. You place your rose.

Take some time there - if you would like to take some reflections as you wait in this place, use this time for that. Tour Guide leaves some time.

It is time now to visit the many other places the Village offers. Please will you prepare by taking your cloth and getting ready for the next visit.

The Town Hall

So, we are going to visit the Town Hall. No one wants to come here. There are papers you must fill out and decisions you must make. Where are all the documents you need? You have to read the small print, talk to officials and sign in black ink with a fountain pen. You have to think of the future when you have no taste for anything other than going to ground. Almost immediately, you have to make decisions. You have to organise a funeral and make arrangements for a grave. There are forms and documents which you often have never seen before. In a moment of shock and confusion, you have to decide on things that often cannot be changed later. These decisions take a lot of energy, the small ones and the large ones. All of them add up, and your energy changes in response.

There are others in the Town Hall, and they seem to be dealing with it differently from you. How is your process through the town hall?

Using your cloth, create a shape or place that represents the activity of The Town Hall.

Take some time there. Make some reflections as you wait in this place
Tour Guide leaves some time.
It is time now to move on. Gather up your cloth and make your way from this place and back into the Village.

The Pub

We then leave the Town Hall and come back into the world outside. As we go out, we hear the sound of laughter and joy coming from a cheery building. Some warm light shines from the windows, and people come and go. There is happiness, community and nothing of loneliness.

The joy may feel intrusive. Why is this here, in my Village of grief? How dare others be so full of life and joy when my loved one is no more? Watch for a moment. Watch how it is to stop grieving for just a moment. Forget the loss for just a minute. Be part of life once more. Be among those people, friends, in joy, as you have been so often before. This place is also part of your Village of grief. It is your longing for life and the reality that others might want to celebrate and be joyful. They have not forgotten, they still might grieve, but days of joy come.

Please don't be angry with them when they need this rest time from grief and mourning. Don't judge yourself when you enjoy these times of rest and refreshment yourself. It is part of your grief. Maybe join them and stay for a while.

Take some time there. Make some reflections as you wait in this place
Tour Guide leaves some time.
It is time now to move on. Gather up your cloth and make your way from this place and back into the Village.

The Smith Shop

Coming out of the pub, you notice the sound of hammers. The clang of beating hot metal can be heard. You find yourself walking to the Smithy.

This is your place of work where you really can hammer things out, sweat, be angry and violent! Here, you can work all you need and do the hard and painful work. You come to this place when you feel that sitting around is insufficient. When your body and your soul cry out for action, you can come here and swing the hammer powerfully.

Fire and bellows are given a place. A place to beat out the feelings. A place where the work of the loss can happen. You move towards the great furnace and, from its heat, beat out a shape from the molten metal that is waiting for you to form it.

Take some time there. Make some reflections as you wait in this place

Tour Guide leaves some time.

It is time now to move on. Gather up your cloth and make your way from this place and back into the Village.

The Sacred Space

We now enter a large, quiet building. Quietness and serenity welcome into the soft light of candles and the warm colours of stained glass windows. There seemed to be music in the air. A deep feeling of peace fills your heart, a sense of peace and quietness.

Here is the quiet place, the place to meditate. And here, you can listen to your heart and that music of your soul. You can ask the hard questions to a Presence attending you. Where do we come from? Where will we go? Why me? And ultimately: Why?

Wait in that place.

Take some time there. Make some reflections as you wait in this place

Tour Guide leaves some time.

It is time now to move on. Gather up your cloth and make your way from this place and back into the Village.

The Hospital

The smell of the next building wafts over. It is an antiseptic, the smell of a hospital, and you go in. There are green walls in long hallways where every step has an echo. There may also be painful memories, but it is also a place of healing.

You are hurt in body, mind and soul. Take your time to feel your wounds, acknowledge them, and let them heal. You have to take good care of yourself. In the time of grief, sometimes your body speaks unclearly to you. You forget to eat, to drink. You have to be your caretaker and nurse and take good care.

People around are being nursed and cared for. Others sit next to them and listen as they tell of their wounds, aches, and pains. Doctors think about the correct treatment. Someone comes to you and offers to tend to you. How do you respond?

Take some time there. Make some reflections as you wait in this place
Tour Guide leaves some time.
It is time now to move on. Gather up your cloth and make your way from this place and back into the Village.

The Shop

Next, we are taken to a small shop.   There needs to be a shop in the Village. Where else should one get all those things one needs? What do you need? What do you desire? The few things you once had in your daily life may feel unneeded now.

But this is not an ordinary shop. Here you can get the things you need. You can find that new flat and job you need now. That smaller car and that smaller stove to make meals just for one. Here you can find those things you wanted to do for so long but couldn't do it. Here you find addresses of groups and meeting places of help and support. Here you can find just what is needed and new skills to reorganise your life.

The things we need are very important, and we must think about them carefully. It is part of grieving to think about one's life and future. Now you have time to visit the Shop and explore what you need and what you can find there on the shelves, waiting for you.

Take some time there. Make some reflections as you wait in this place
Tour Guide leaves some time.
It is time now to move on. Gather up your cloth and make your way from this place and back into the Village.

The Cemetery

Now the day is a little darker day, and we wander over to the cemetery. A heavy iron gate with ivy growing on the bars guards the entrance. Under dark skies, the calling of an owl, flying under the low branches of a weeping willow, can be heard. It is cold, and the forest's thorns can be felt all around. Find a place here.

It is a dark place, yes, a place of mourning and fear, of unknown horrors hiding in the darkness between the graves. But you must come here to meet your fears, all that scares you, in death and life. See what it is that scares and frightens you so that you can deal with it.

This cemetery is a place of memories and reconnection. It could be a picture on the wall with whom we talk. Or the empty chair that will remain forever theirs. It can be a place where we can see our loved one sitting with us during long and lonely evenings.

Take some time there. Make some reflections as you wait in this place
Tour Guide leaves some time.
It is time now to move on. Gather up your cloth and make your way from this place and back into the Village.

The Oracle

Lastly, after leaving the cemetery, we make our way to The Oracle Place, which is hard to see unless you have eyes that see in the darkness. It's a kind of Post Office, except this place conveys invisible messages. If you come towards it, there is a gift waiting for you. You will be met here in a half-seeing way. The being or thing that you lost will find you there. They are waiting.

They will not meet you through everyday consciousness – they will meet you in a song you hear. Or a half-formed image. Or a dream. It may be that a bird catches your attention, comes close and watches you. Or that a feather drops from the sky. It may be a felt sense of the beloved or something you need to hear from the thing you have lost suddenly takes up residence in you. Your brain may not compute it, but your skin and soul recognise it. It may be a tingle, a vibration, a sound.

Come to the oracle ready to hear. Sit down in its energy. What do you hear? What can be half-seen? And will you let the eyes of imagination take you one step closer to that sense?

Take some time there. Make some reflections as you wait in this place
Tour Guide leaves sometimes.
It is time to leave now. Gather your cloth and return to the Village Square, where I will meet you.

As you make your way back, notice other people walking around. Some you may know are glad to be grieving with you. But there are others - strange people. They walked around blindfolded or with their hands in front of their eyes. Some of them walk insecurely, reaching around to find obstacles in their way. They don't fall or hurt themselves but hardly move from their spot.

Others walk briskly as if they can see, but they only walk in circles, bumping into things and people, hurting themselves and others.

Just notice them – the people avoiding their grief- knowing its reason but declaring that it has no connection with them. They use words like "*he fell asleep,*" "*she moved on,*" or "*we are just grateful that she does not have to suffer anymore.*" They are walking blindfolded.

Just notice as you return to the Village Square where I am waiting for you.

Leave some time till everyone comes back. If anyone loiters, use the Tour Guide's voice to bring them back. "*We need to gather again now – this place is always open, so you can come back whenever you need to. This is not a once-in-a-lifetime visit*".
When everyone is back

We are just about to leave the Village and make our way back. You now know that The Village of Grief can be visited over and over. It will take a long, long time before you will have the desire to walk away entirely. You alone can decide when you will go, how far you'll walk, how fast you'll travel. Nobody will force you out of this place. For this is your Village of Grief.

Begin to make your way along the pathway out of The Village, back into the forest and through the trees. The forest now seems less old and dark. You find yourself in the meadow and countryside, and the day is still warm. The Village will always be there for your return. No one can take this from you, ever.

Let people find their way back to the room.
Derole the process by noticing they are back in the room —
Notice colours in the room and people.
Ask them to shake out their material so it becomes an everyday bit of cloth again.
Invite them to brush off anything they do not want to keep from The Village journey and hold onto anything important.

Meet in a standing circle and go around the circle asking for one word from each person.

Give some time for them to make notes.

Process either in the large group together or in smaller groups.

Ending ritual for the whole group, e.g., standing in a circle and offering a blessing word to the others on the bereavement journey.

One to One work

The Village of Grief can also be used in one-to-one sessions working with miniatures of The Village locations. The pictures below shows work done with a client when we created their Village and then made the journey. The pictures are used with permission.

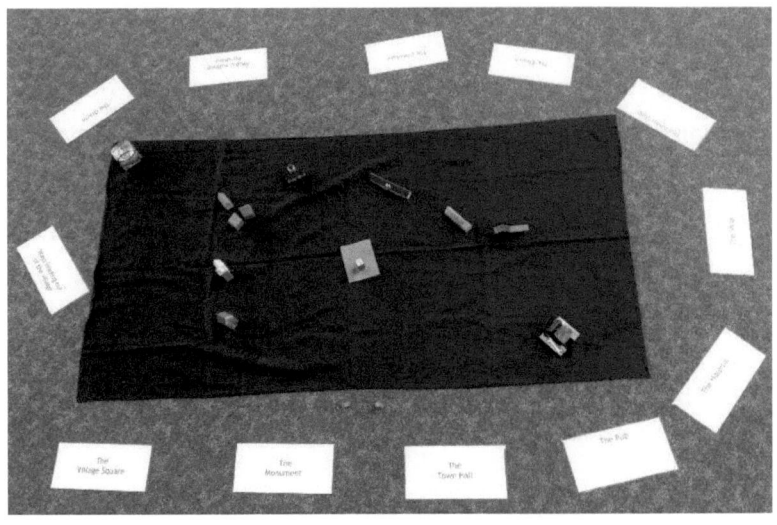

About the Authors

Rev. Dr. Axel Schwaigert

Reverend Doctor Axel Schwaigert, Stuttgart, Baden-Württemberg (Germany), received his Diplom in Evangelische Theologie (Diploma in Protestant Theology) from the School of Theological Studies at Tübingen (Germany) and studied inter-religious dialogue at Temple University in Philadelphia, PA. He began his pastoral training in 1998 at MCC Bournemouth (UK). In 2000 he launched the new Salz der Erde MCC Stuttgart (Germany) during Gay Pride. After 10 years of building this new congregation in surroundings not familiar with independent churches, Axel went on to earn his Doctor of Ministry degree at Episcopal Divinity School in Cambridge, MA (USA). His thesis was on "Communual Grief in Relationship to HIV/AIDS"

In his secular life, Axel works as a funeral director.

He loves singing, dancing, and acting on stage in musicals, which he sometimes dares at a community theater of the US Forces in Stuttgart.

Mary Smail

I trained as a Sesame Drama and Movement Therapy in 1990 and used movement, story, and imagination for ten years to help people become more themselves. Examples where I worked as a Dramatherapist include:

Children survivors of abuse (St Christopher's Fellowship)
Adults with Learning Difficulties (NHS)
Adults in mental health care (Chapel Orchard Centre)
Elders in residential and daycare (Roundabout)
One to one Dramatherapy with adults (Private Practice)

In 2006, after completing a counselling course at the Westminster Pastoral Foundation, I trained with Re-Vision www.re-vision.org.uk/ and graduated as a psychotherapist.

 I am a Scot with strong ties to Ireland and all things Celtic. The way that people come to life, even in the direst of situations, inspires me, along with a deep belief that however hard a situation appears, something new will eventually emerge.

I am a singer, songwriter, and storyteller and have lifelong experience using the folk arts within spiritual contexts. Dear, to my heart has been the place of the folk arts in liturgy within the Christian church.

My present special area of interest is to explore areas of creativity with people in the last stages of life, with Alzheimer's, or in a bereavement process.

In addition, I have two black cats and a sunken garden, full of flowers.